Just a Song at Twilight

A Play

Valerie Maskell

A SAMUEL FRENCH ACTING EDITION

SAMUEL FRENCH

FOUNDED 1830

SAMUELFRENCH-LONDON.CO.UK
SAMUELFRENCH.COM

JUST A SONG AT TWILIGHT is fully protected under the copyright laws of the British Commonwealth, including Canada, the United States of America, and all other countries of the Copyright Union. All rights, including professional and amateur stage productions, recitation, lecturing, public reading, motion picture, radio broadcasting, television and the rights of translation into foreign languages are strictly reserved.

ISBN 978-0-573-02348-4

www.samuelfrench-london.co.uk

www.samuelfrench.com

FOR AMATEUR PRODUCTION ENQUIRIES

UNITED KINGDOM AND WORLD
EXCLUDING NORTH AMERICA
plays@SamuelFrench-London.co.uk
020 7255 4302/01

Each title is subject to availability from Samuel French,

depending upon country of performance.

CAUTION: Professional and amateur producers are hereby warned that *JUST A SONG AT TWILIGHT* is subject to a licensing fee. Publication of this play does not imply availability for performance. Both amateurs and professionals considering a production are strongly advised to apply to the appropriate agent before starting rehearsals, advertising, or booking a theatre. A licensing fee must be paid whether the title is presented for charity or gain and whether or not admission is charged.

The professional rights in this play are controlled by Samuel French Ltd, 52 Fitzroy Street, London, W1T 5JR.

No one shall make any changes in this title for the purpose of production. No part of this book may be reproduced, stored in a retrieval system, or transmitted in any form, by any means, now known or yet to be invented, including mechanical, electronic, photocopying, recording, videotaping, or otherwise, without the prior written permission of the publisher. No one shall upload this title, or part of this title, to any social media websites.

The right of Valerie Maskell to be identified as author of this work has been asserted by her in accordance with Section 77 of the Copyright, Designs and Patents Act 1988

CHARACTERS

Mrs Barker
Miss Pratt
Miss Hamilton
Nurse
First Vicar
Second Vicar

The action takes place in an Old People's Home

Time—the present

JUST A SONG AT TWILIGHT

An open stage, with no scenery

The three old ladies are seated in chairs (preferably, but not necessarily, wheelchairs), with Miss Pratt in the centre, Mrs Barker to her right and Mrs Hamilton to her left. Miss Pratt is very old, and the most ga-ga of the three. Her short grey hair is parted on the side and held back with a slide. She is cocooned in shawls. Mrs Barker is also very old, well over eighty. She has sparse white hair scraped back, and wears a masculine wool dressing-gown. Mrs Hamilton has grey hair, quite nicely waved. She is fully dressed in a cardigan over a blouse, but has a rug over her knees like the others

The only other furniture is a small table with thermometers, medicines, notebooks, and similar necessities

As the Lights come up the old ladies are dozing. Mrs Barker opens her eyes suddenly, glares round, and speaks

Mrs Barker That's the third time we've had stew this week.

Mrs Hamilton wakes up, and begins to read a large-print book. Miss Pratt opens her eyes and blinks vaguely

Disgusting muck.

Miss Pratt Why don't you tell her about it?

Mrs Barker Who?

Miss Pratt The cook. Why don't you get rid of her?

Mrs Barker (*irritably*) Because it's not my house.

Miss Pratt I can't think why you keep her on. Is she a relation of yours?

Mrs Barker (*furiously, leaning towards Miss Pratt*) It's not my house! We're IN A HOME! I've told you a hundred times. God give me patience.

Miss Pratt begins to whimper

Nurse enters. She is young, brisk, kind

Nurse Now what is all this? Oh, Mrs Barker, you haven't upset her again? What's the matter, dear?
Miss Pratt I'm going home. (*She throws off her rug*)
Nurse You can't go home today, dear.
Mrs Barker Or any other day.

Nurse tucks in Miss Pratt. Mrs Barker heaves an angry sigh

Mrs Hamilton You really are the limit, Agnes. Poor old thing.
Mrs Barker Poor old thing! She's no older than me, or you.
Mrs Hamilton It's not a question of age ...
Mrs Barker Isn't it? That's what you think. Everything's a question of age. We're here because we're old and we're going to die. The sooner she gets that into her head the better.
Mrs Hamilton You speak for yourself. I've been feeling quite well lately. (*She takes out some coarse knitting, on huge needles. It is a dishcloth*)
Mrs Barker What on earth is that you're doing?
Mrs Hamilton Knitting.
Mrs Barker I can see that, but what?
Mrs Hamilton A dishcloth, as a matter of fact.

Mrs Barker snorts offensively

I like to keep occupied. I can't read for long at a time.
Mrs Barker At our time of life if you can't do anything better than knit dishcloths you may as well do nothing at all.
Nurse Now do stop arguing. Have you forgotten what day it is today? It's Thursday! You know who comes on Thursday.
Mrs Barker All the days are the same here.
Mrs Hamilton I haven't forgotten. It's Thursday, Agnes. The Vicar's day!
Mrs Barker He needn't bother to come and see me.

Mrs Hamilton fumbles in her handbag

Mrs Hamilton My lipstick—it must be here somewhere—ah.

Nurse holds a small mirror while Mrs Hamilton shakily applies a bright red lipstick

Mrs Barker Lipstick at her age. It's indecent.
Nurse (*to Mrs Hamilton*) Shall I comb your hair?
Mrs Hamilton I can do it.

She does so, but Nurse puts the finishing touches

Mrs Barker Ridiculous fuss!
Nurse (*to Miss Pratt, loudly*) The Vicar's coming this morning, dear. That will be nice, won't it? You always like to see the Vicar.
Miss Pratt (*throwing off her blanket*) I've got to get some shopping done.
Nurse (*holding her down firmly*) Don't worry about that now. Come on, let me make you nice and tidy.
Mrs Barker Can't think why he bothers. None of us have been to church for thirty years.
Mrs Hamilton He's a very kind, nice man.
Miss Pratt (*to Nurse*) Dorothy! Dorothy! Has Mother gone to sleep?
Nurse Yes, fast asleep.
Miss Pratt I suppose I'd better make sure. (*Once more she tries to get out of her chair*)
Nurse Now, dear, don't try to get up. You know you mustn't . . .

Miss Pratt pinches Nurse viciously on the arm

Oh!
Mrs Hamilton Oh dear! Oh, Nurse, I'm afraid she hurt you!
Nurse (*controlling herself with an effort, rubbing her arm*) It was nothing. All in the day's work.
Mrs Barker I don't call it nothing. It's time she was painlessly put down. Time we were all put down.
Mrs Hamilton Agnes, really!
Mrs Barker If we were dogs, we would be put down. I never kept a dog to be a misery to itself.
Mrs Hamilton My little Tiggie lived to be nearly seventeen.
Mrs Barker Poor little horror. Must have stunk to high heaven.
Mrs Hamilton Even if he did, I still loved him.
Mrs Barker Deaf, incontinent, and paralyzed in it's back legs—like her.
Miss Pratt Dorothy, do you hear? That's Mother's bell.
Nurse (*busy at the table, her back to the old woman*) I didn't hear it.
Miss Pratt (*shrewishly*) Well I did. There's none so deaf as them that won't hear.

Nurse (*stonily, in a dreary, tired voice*) I'm not deaf, Nell, and I didn't hear it.

Miss Pratt Well, make sure. Go on. Go and make sure.

Nurse I'm tired, Nell. I've been up and down stairs all morning.

Miss Pratt Tired. You're tired. Lazy is what you are, always were. Fat and lazy! And you don't love Mother.

Nurse (*tearfully*) I do. I do, Nell. Of course I love Mother.

Miss Pratt (*triumphantly*) No you don't. You don't love Mother like I do! (*Pause*) THAT was her bell that time, anyway.

Nurse Couldn't you go, Nell? Just for once. I haven't finished my dinner . . .

Miss Pratt Fat! Lazy! You don't love Mother.

Nurse I'll go. I'll go.

Nurse goes off, with a weary sigh

Miss Pratt If it weren't for me, no-one would bother about Mother. If it weren't for me, she'd be left to die. (*Self-satisfied, she sinks back into torpor*)

Mrs Hamilton It sounds to me as though Dorothy had a wretched time of it.

Mrs Barker Expect she deserved it. No backbone. Ought to have stood up for herself.

Nurse enters

Nurse (*cheerfully*) Mr Reed is coming up the drive.

Miss Pratt gradually slips down in her chair

Mrs Barker Can't stand vicars. They're all humbugs.

Nurse Now do mind what you say, Mrs Barker.

Mrs Barker Can't think what you see in him. Yard of pump-water.

Mrs Hamilton Agnes, you're very rude. I'm sure he's very nice. I like a tall man myself.

Mrs Barker I'm sick of hearing about the Vicar. Anyone would think he was the only man in the world.

Mrs Hamilton He *is* the only man in our world. And we like him, don't we, Nurse? I think he likes you too, dear, I do really. I'm sure he's going to ask you out. Shall you go?

Nurse He hasn't asked me yet.
Mrs Hamilton But he's working up to it, I can see that.
Mrs Barker You might as well go out and enjoy yourself, if you get the chance. You'll be a long time dead, like the rest of us . . .

Nurse heaves Miss Pratt up

That one won't last much longer.
Mrs Hamilton Agnes!
Mrs Barker Well, why not face facts? One of us has got to go first. Not that I'd mind if it was me. I'm in agony with my leg. Nobody gives a damn. If I was a horse I'd have me shot.
Nurse (*laughing*) Honestly, Mrs Barker, the things you say . . .

The first Vicar enters, a tall, thin young man, who cloaks his extreme shyness under a hearty manner

Vicar Hello, ladies! How are we all this morning?
Mrs Barker Dying.
Mrs Hamilton We're very well, thank you.
Vicar (*to Mrs Hamilton*) You're looking very smart. Is that a new blouse?
Mrs Hamilton Why, fancy you noticing that! Did you hear that, Agnes? The Vicar noticed my blouse. No, it's not new, I've had it by me for quite a while, and I thought today, why not wear it? What am I waiting for? So Nurse found it in my suitcase and helped me to put it on. Didn't you, dear? You see, we have to keep things in our suitcases, in the luggage room, because there's no space in the ward. I often think how nice it would be just to have a little chest of drawers of my own. Then I could keep a few things on the top, photographs, you know, and a little vase of flowers; things like that. I had a window-box once, before I came here. That was when I had that little flat, after Henry passed away. Everybody was so sorry for me, losing my husband so suddenly, and having to leave The Cedars. But they needn't have been, you know, I didn't mind a bit, leaving The Cedars, I mean. It was such a big house, with those cold high rooms, yes, seven bedrooms it had, and a huge garden. Henry's family had money, you know, I remember how pleased my mother was, when we

were engaged. Well . . . Oh, dear, I've forgotten what I was going to say.

Mrs Barker Thank heaven for small mercies.

Nurse (*encouragingly*) You were telling us about your window-box.

Mrs Hamilton Oh, yes. Well, it was really lovely in the spring, everyone admired it, but the wood rotted, and I was so afraid it would fall down and hurt someone, I had to get it dismantled, so old Mr Francis, he lived next door you know—his mother made dresses for Queen Victoria . . . (*She hesitates, losing the threads*)

Vicar (*without taking his eyes off Nurse, at whom he has been looking all this time*) Well, well, fancy that. Queen Victoria, eh. What a splendid thing.

Mrs Barker Damn fool.

Vicar (*still gazing at Nurse*) A splendid thing, a many-splendoured thing.

Mrs Hamilton (*looking straight ahead. In a younger, more timid voice*) Harry, dear, I've been wondering—that bit of garden by the potting-shed, it doesn't seem to be used for anything, and I wondered if . . .

Vicar (*in a deep voice, still looking at Nurse*) Just a minute, Edith.

Mrs Hamilton I'd like to grow some flowers of my own—I could get some packets of seeds from Woolworths, they do look so nice and bright——

Vicar (*interrupting brusquely*) What do you think Perkins is for?

Mrs Hamilton Oh, he's a wonderful gardener, I know, it always looks perfect—it's just that . . .

Vicar Leave it to him, then. You don't want to go messing about in the garden when you've got a gardener. Leave it to Perkins. Understand?

Mrs Hamilton (*meekly*) Yes, Henry.

Vicar (*to Nurse*) Stupid bitch. Wanting to make mud pies at her age.

Nurse (*in a coy, sugary voice; looking up at him*) You're not very nice to her, Henry.

Vicar Never mind. You be nice to me, eh?

Nurse giggles

Miss Pratt Dorothy! Dorothy! Where is she? Never here when she's wanted. Dorothy!

Mrs Barker Live in the past, that's all they do. Not that I blame them. It couldn't be worse than the present. My horses had more comfort than we do, and better medical attention. (*To the Vicar*) Doctor, when are you going to look at my leg? It's agony, it really is. (*She throws off her blanket showing a bandaged leg*)

Nurse She thinks you're the doctor. She wants you to look at her leg.

Vicar (*kindly*) I'm not the doctor, Mrs Barker. I'm the Vicar. You remember me. We could pray for your leg together, if you like.

Mrs Barker It doesn't need prayer, it needs a poultice!

Vicar Prayer is a kind of poultice.

Mrs Barker Don't talk rubbish!

Nurse I'll see to your leg, dear, now don't worry the Vicar.

Vicar (*rather wearily*) May the blessing of God be upon you all. (*Moving away with Nurse*) I wonder if I do any good, coming here. They hardly know who I am.

Nurse Of course you do good. It makes a very nice change for them, seeing you.

Vicar And you? Does it make a nice change for you?

Nurse I'd go daft if you stopped coming. Cooped up here with them all the time. Oh, I'm quite fond of them, you know, they're just like children. But they're no company.

Vicar Look, I was wondering—would you—how about coming to tea when you have an afternoon off? My mother lives with me, you know—she'd so like to meet you. I've told her a lot about you.

Nurse Well . . .

Vicar Do say you'll come, we'll have tea in the garden, and strawberries. Strawberries and cream.

Nurse Thank you, I'd like to come very much. It's my Sunday off this week, I could come then.

Vicar And we'll walk across to the church together for Evensong. Four o'clock at the Vicarage. I must go. Good-bye, Mrs Hamilton. Good-bye, Miss Pratt. Good-bye, Mrs Barker.

He approaches each one in turn. Miss Pratt pinches him, the others shake hands

The first Vicar exits

Mrs Barker Thank the Lord he's gone.
Mrs Hamilton Did he say anything, Nurse?
Nurse He's asked me to tea. His mother will be there.
Mrs Hamilton His mother. That's a good sign.

*The Lights dim over the old ladies, who doze off. Nurse moves
forward into a Spot*

Nurse I'll wear my blue dress with the full sleeves, and my new
    shoes, and we'll sit round a table under a tree, drinking tea,
    and being polite, and then we'll walk to Church, just us two,
    hand in hand. And I'll climb over the stile and sit on the top
    of it, with the skirt of my blue dress spread out around me,
    and I shall be laughing, and the sun will shine through my
    hair. I must wash my hair, and iron my dress, and that is how
    it will be.

*The Lights dim to indicate the passage of time. Nurse stands
quite still, the old ladies sleep in half-light for about three seconds.
The Lights come up slowly. Nurse moves to Mrs Barker, covers
her tidily, to Miss Pratt and pulls up a woolly shawl round her
head, and buttons a cardigan for Mrs Hamilton. By the time this
is finished the Lights are full on and the old ladies wake up*

Mrs Hamilton Are you off this afternoon, Nurse?
Nurse Yes, I'm going to the Vicarage to tea.
Mrs Hamilton Oh, that'll be nice. Do you hear that, Agnes?
    Nurse is going to tea at the Vicarage.
Mrs Barker Rather her than me.
Mrs Hamilton Well, that needn't worry you. He's not likely to
    ask a rude old woman like you to tea, is he, Nurse?
Nurse She doesn't mean it, do you, Mrs Barker?
Mrs Barker Of course I mean it. Just because I'm old, do I have
    to spend all my time saying things I don't mean? That's just
    where you're wrong. I do say what I mean, exactly what I
    mean. I wouldn't go to tea with the Vicar if he was the last
    man on earth. Neither would Nurse if he wasn't the only
    thing in trousers she ever sets eyes on.
Mrs Hamilton You're very vulgar, Agnes. It's very trying to me

being cooped up here with someone so vulgar. I wasn't brought
up to that kind of talk.
Mrs Barker You were brought up not to say boo to a goose. I
say what I think. It's one of the privileges of age. When I see
a goose I say BOO! (*She bellows the word in Miss Pratt's
direction*)

*Miss Pratt wakes with a violent start and tries to get out of her
chair*

Miss Pratt Dorothy! Where are you? Dorothy!

Nurse goes to her

Nurse Now, dear, it's all right, there's nothing wrong. I wish
you wouldn't do that kind of thing, Mrs Barker. She might
have had a heart attack.
Miss Pratt Where's my tea?
Nurse It's not teatime yet. It's coffee time. I'll go and get you
all a nice cup of coffee. Now be good while I've gone, I won't be
a minute.

Nurse goes off

Mrs Hamilton That's a nice girl, you know. We're lucky to have
her.
Mrs Barker She's not a bad sort of girl, I suppose. God knows
why else she wants to waste her time looking after us.
Mrs Hamilton You're thoroughly ungrateful. Where should we
be without people like her?
Mrs Barker In the grave. And a good thing too.
Mrs Hamilton Sometimes, Agnes, you're so morbid it is almost
more than I can bear.
Miss Pratt Where's Dorothy? Where's Dorothy gone? It's time
for Mother's tablets. Has she gone down to the library?
Mrs Barker (*to Miss Pratt, loudly*) Dorothy's not here! She's
gone and she's not coming back!
Miss Pratt Why?
Mrs Barker Because she had enough of *you*, that's why. Poor
bitch.
Mrs Hamilton (*warningly*) Agnes!

Nurse enters, carrying a small tray with coffee. She puts it down on the table, and bursts into tears

Mrs Barker and Mrs Hamilton are concerned

Mrs Hamilton What is it, dear? What happened?
Mrs Barker Come on. Come on. No use crying over spilt milk. Have you broken a thermometer?
Nurse (*stifling sobs*) No. It's Michael—Mr Reed—the Vicar. He's been in a car accident.
Mrs Hamilton Is he hurt?
Nurse He's dead. He died at once. (*She turns away, weeping quietly*)
Mrs Hamilton (*after a pause*) How very sad.
Mrs Barker (*cheerfully*) It's a tragedy. Nothing more nor less than a tragedy.
Mrs Hamilton A good man like that.
Mrs Barker So sudden.
Mrs Hamilton So very sudden.
Miss Pratt Has something happened? Is it Mother?
Mrs Hamilton And so young.
Mrs Barker So very young.
Mrs Hamilton It just goes to show.
Mrs Barker You never really know.

Mrs Hamilton and Mrs Barker exchange a conspiratorial look. Then they jump up and out of their chairs, and begin a macabre dance, jigging and hopping about, ugly and ungainly but very lively, like two old witches. As they dance they sing the following words to a jingly tune. The singing and dancing can be divided up at the discretion of the director

SONG

You never know, you never know
The one that will be first to go
It may not be the one that's ill
For anyone can have a spill
It may not be the one that's old
For anyone can catch a cold
Lift up your hearts, forget your fear,
For he is gone, but we're still here!

Finishing on a note of triumph, Mrs Hamilton and Mrs Barker return to their chairs, smiling. They are not puffed or tired, since this has not really happened: it is simply an abstraction of how they feel. They settle in their chairs, and fall into a doze

The Lights dim slowly. All the old ladies sleep

Nurse pushes Miss Pratt off in her wheelchair, and returns

The Lights come up. Mrs Barker is now sunk in torpor, Mrs Hamilton is busy knitting her dishcloth, and Nurse is writing at the table

Mrs Hamilton It's an awful thing to say, but Agnes is much easier to live with since that last funny turn.
Nurse It's taken it out of her a lot, but still, I daresay she'll buck up again. It's amazing how people do.
Mrs Hamilton You've had some bucking up of your own to do, haven't you, dear? I know how fond you were of the dear Vicar.
Nurse Poor Michael.
Mrs Hamilton A quiet young man, but very nice.
Nurse If he'd lived, he'd never have been able to walk again.
Mrs Hamilton Nature knows best. That's what I always say.
Mrs Barker (*with a flash of her old self*) Nature's a fool.

The second Vicar enters: dark, stocky, healthy looking, young

Vicar (*very heartily*) Hello, there, hello, hello, hello! I'm the new Vicar. Just popping in to make myself known. Hello, Nurse. Very pleased to meet you. Now, this is Mrs . . .
Mrs Hamilton Hamilton. How do you do, Vicar? And this is Mrs Barker.
Vicar Mrs Hamilton and Mrs Barker. Now, I must remember that. What are you knitting, Mrs Hamilton?
Mrs Hamilton Just a dishcloth. It's all I can manage nowadays. But they're very useful. They're always glad of them in the kitchen.
Vicar Very praiseworthy, Mrs Hamilton. Now that is a fine dishcloth. I tell you what, I'll get you to make one for me. I could do with a new dishcloth—last one I had was a bit of an old

vest. Ha ha! Lucky the Bishop doesn't inspect the kitchen, eh?

Mrs Hamilton (*pleased*) I'll do one for you with pleasure.

Mrs Barker (*coming to life a bit*) Common young man. Who's that common young man? Has he come to buy a dog?

Vicar Ha, ha, you've got a right one there, Nurse. I shall have to mind my Ps and Qs around here, I can see that. Well, I must be off. I'll see you again soon. Now, don't forget that dishcloth.

Mrs Hamilton Good-bye, Vicar. Of course I shan't forget.

Mrs Barker Where's he going?

Vicar (*privately, to Nurse*) Now, what do you do with your time off? How about coming up to the Vicarage for a cup of tea next time you're off duty? Bring your bikini if the sun's shining, eh? Or even if it's not, ha, ha.

The Light on the wheelchairs dims. Mrs Barker dozes. Mrs Hamilton knits. Nurse and the Vicar move downstage in a Spot

Nurse I haven't got a bikini.

Vicar You'll have to get one. There's a lovely sheltered spot in the garden, and a bottle of lemon and lime in the fridge.

Nurse I'll think about it.

Vicar Tomorrow afternoon.

Nurse I'm not off till Monday.

Vicar Monday then. About three.

The Vicar goes

The Spot fades on Nurse, and comes up on Mrs Hamilton

Mrs Hamilton What a nice young man. Not like Mr Reed. But Mr Reed died. And now it's Mr Whatsisname. The new one. I don't suppose it will make much difference. Nurse will go to tea at the Vicarage just the same, and I shall knit them a dish-cloth.

The Spot comes up on Nurse, and fades on Mrs Hamilton

Nurse Now that's the kind of man I like. You know where you are with a man like that. I *shall* get a bikini. I shall get a bikini as soon as I can. Mavis is off-duty this afternoon. She can go into town on the bus and get me a bikini and tomorrow afternoon I'll be lying in the sun in the Vicarage garden, and the new Vicar will bring me lemon and lime in a tall glass with lumps of ice, and I'll get brown all over, and I'll leave here and lie in the sun forever, in my bikini, in the Vicarage garden. (*She stands motionless*)

The Lights fade. We hear the voices of the two old women, increasing in volume and raucousness, singing their song. When this is over the Lights go up brilliantly on a stage from which everybody and everything has disappeared, that is to say, the old ladies, their chairs, Nurse and the table

There must be no CURTAIN *call*

FURNITURE AND PROPERTY LIST

On stage: 3 wheelchairs. *On them:* rugs
Small table. *On it:* thermometers, medicine bottles, notebook, pencil, various medical necessities. These items could be glued to a tray to facilitate quick, silent striking

Off stage: Tray with 3 cups of cocoa (**Nurse**)

Personal: **Mrs Hamilton:** large-print book, half-knitted dishcloth and large needles, handbag with comb, mirror and lipstick

LIGHTING PLOT

Property fittings required: nil

An open stage

To open: Black-out

Cue 1	At start of play *Bring up full general lighting*	(**Page** 1)
Cue 2	**Mrs Hamilton**: "That's a good sign." *Dim lighting on wheelchairs, bring up Spot on* **Nurse** *down* C	(**Page** 8)
Cue 3	**Nurse**: ". . . how it will be." *Fade Spot, retain dim lighting for 3 seconds, then return slowly to full*	(**Page** 8)
Cue 4	**Old Ladies** doze after dance *Lights dim*	(**Page** 11)
Cue 5	**Nurse** starts writing at table *Bring up to opening lighting*	(**Page** 11)
Cue 6	**Vicar**: "Or even if it's not, ha, ha." *Fade lighting on wheelchairs, bring up Spot on* **Nurse** *and* **Vicar** *down* C	(**Page** 12)
Cue 7	**Vicar** exits *Crossfade to wheelchair lighting*	(**Page** 12)
Cue 8	**Mrs Hamilton**: ". . . knit them a dishcloth." *Crossfade to Spot on* **Nurse**	(**Page** 12)
Cue 9	**Nurse**: ". . . in the Vicarage garden." *Fade to Black-out*	(**Page** 13)
Cue 10	At end of song, when stage is empty *Snap up brilliant overall lighting*	(**Page** 13)

Lively
rall

www.ingramcontent.com/pod-product-compliance
Ingram Content Group UK Ltd.
Pitfield, Milton Keynes, MK11 3LW, UK
UKHW021818150726
7214IPUK00017B/195